Santa Coloring Book for kids

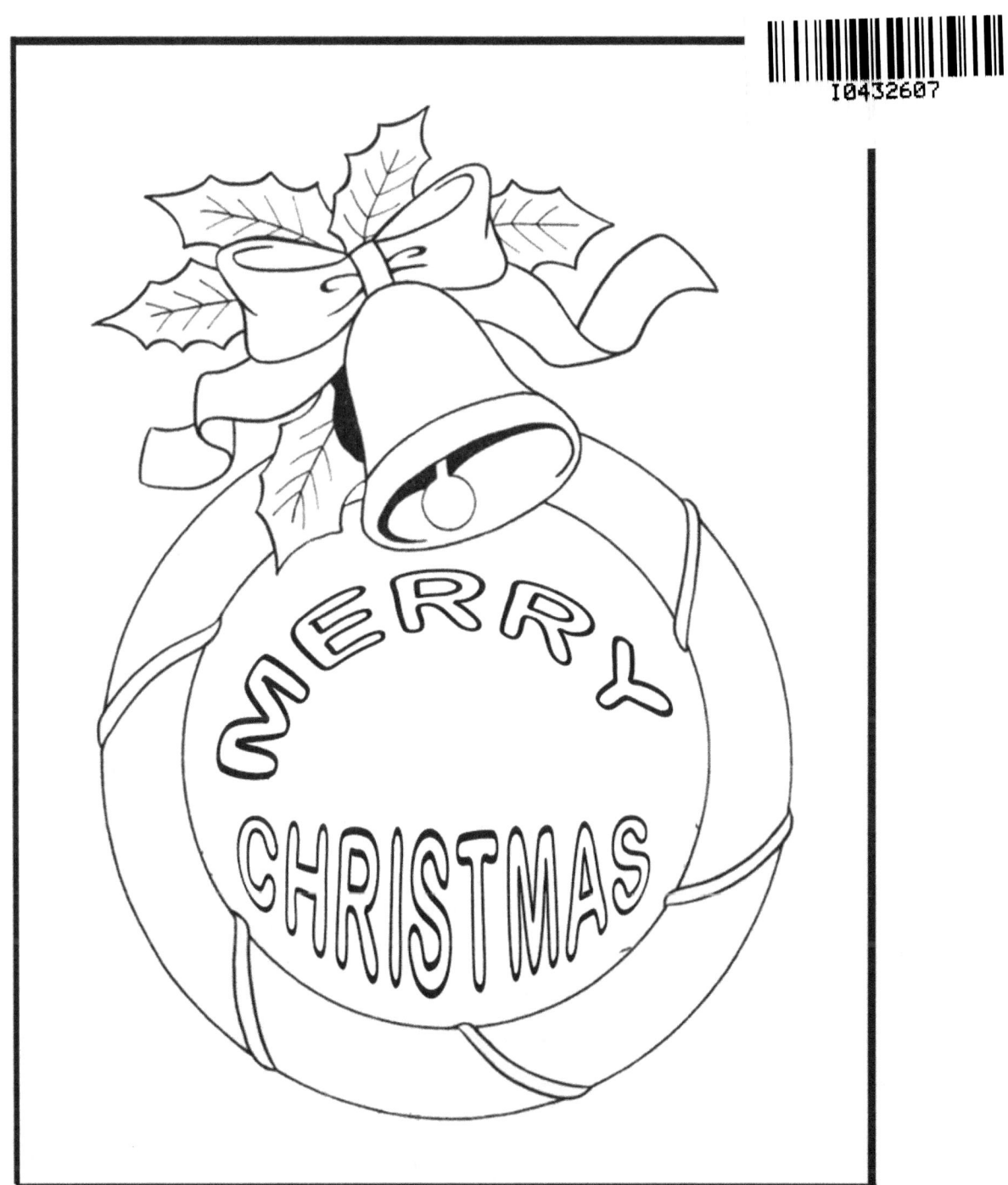

Nina Watson

Santa Coloring Book For Kids

For Kids

Copyright: Published in the United States by **Nina Watson**
Published November 2017

All rights reserved. No part of this publication may be reproduced, stored in retrieval system, copied in any form or by any means, electronic, mechanical, photocopying, recording or otherwise transmitted without written permission from the publisher. Please do not participate in or encourage piracy of this material in any way. You must not circulate this book in any format Nina Watson does not control or direct users' actions and is not responsible for the information or content shared, harm and/or actions of the book readers.

ISBN-13: 978-1979803366

ISBN-10: 1979803366

Santa Claus, also known as **Saint Nicholas, Saint Nick, Kris Kringle, Father Christmas**, or simply **Santa** is a legendary figure of Western Christian culture who is said to bring gifts to the homes of well-behaved ("good" or "nice") children on Christmas Eve (24 December) and the early morning hours of Christmas Day (25 December)

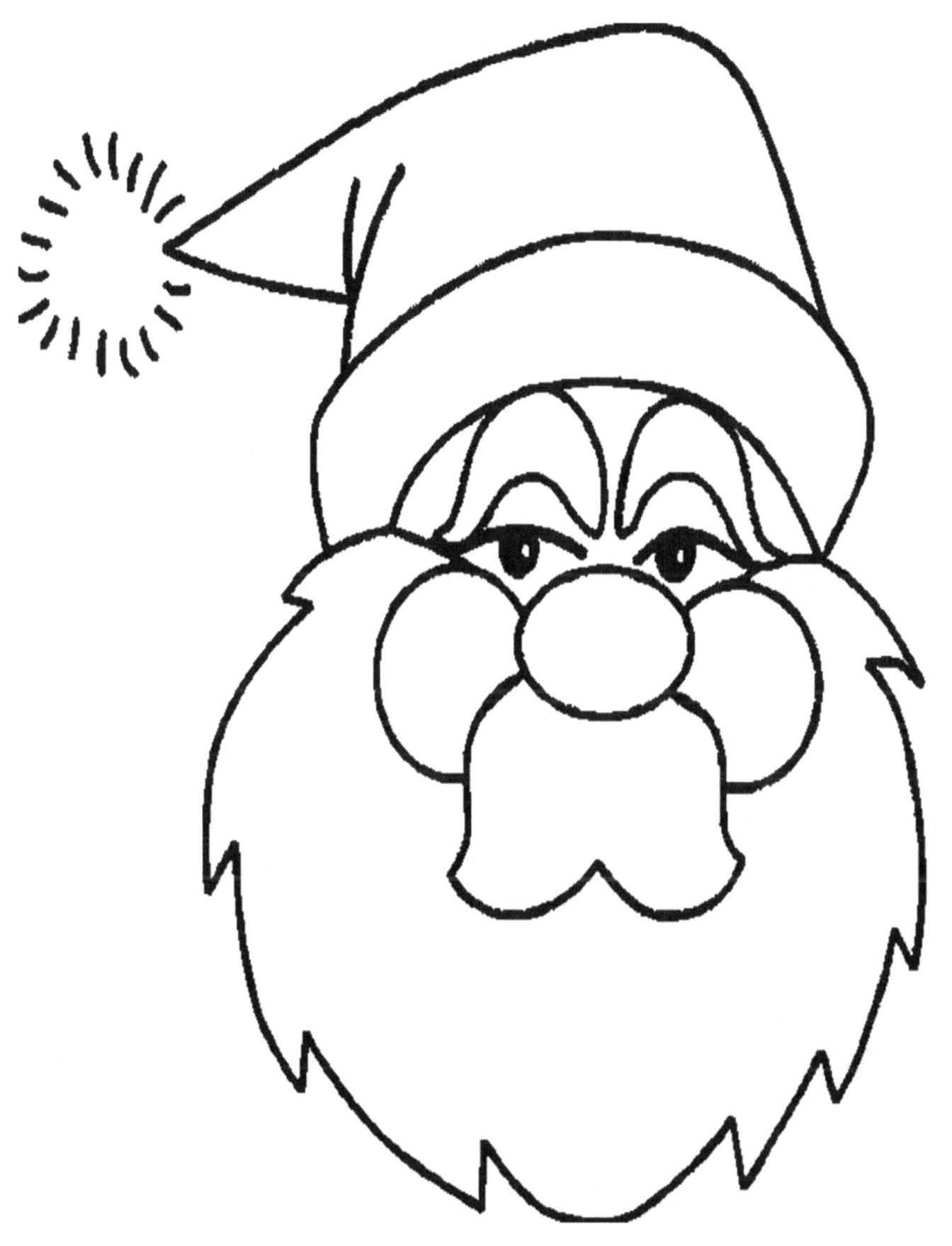

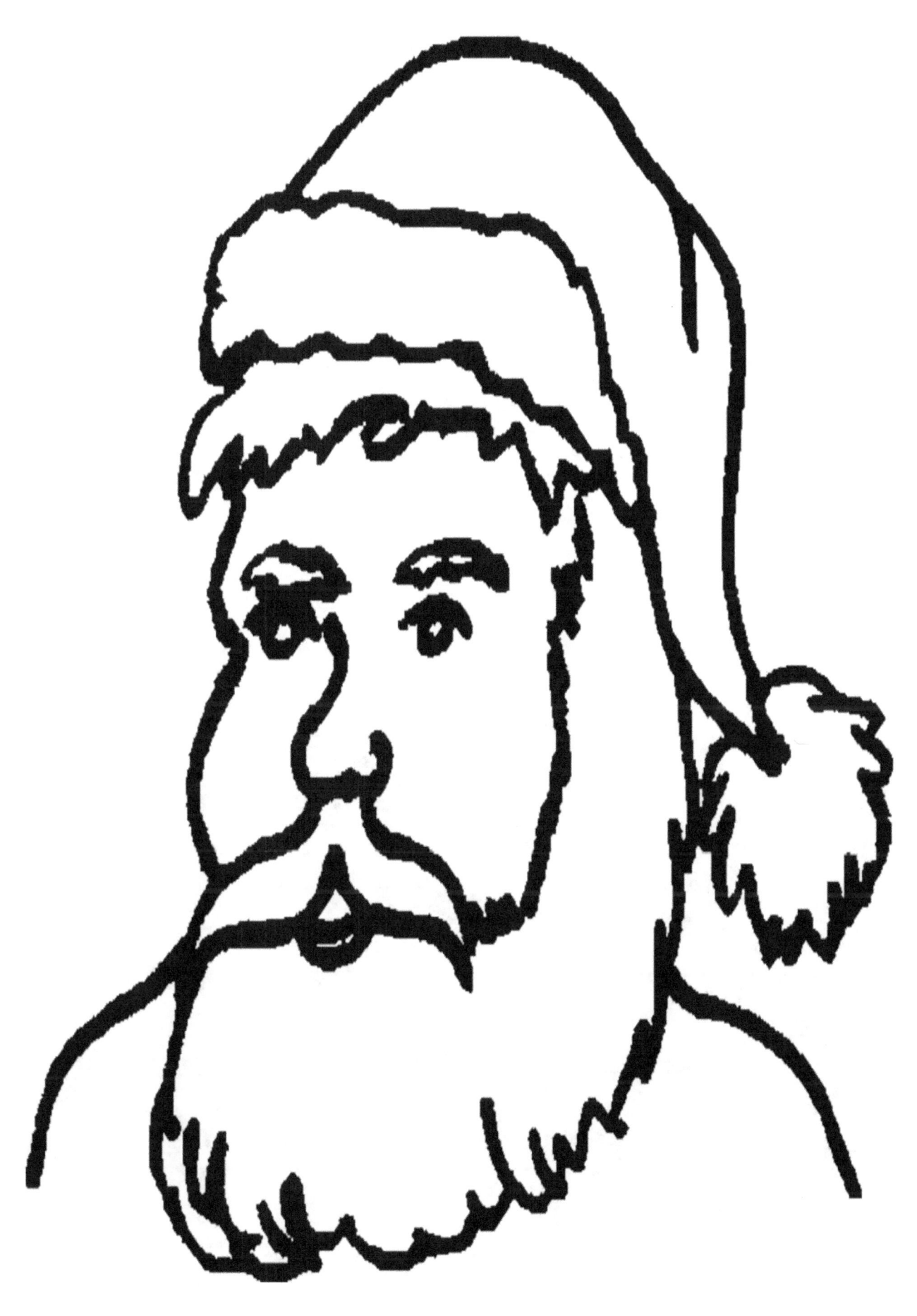

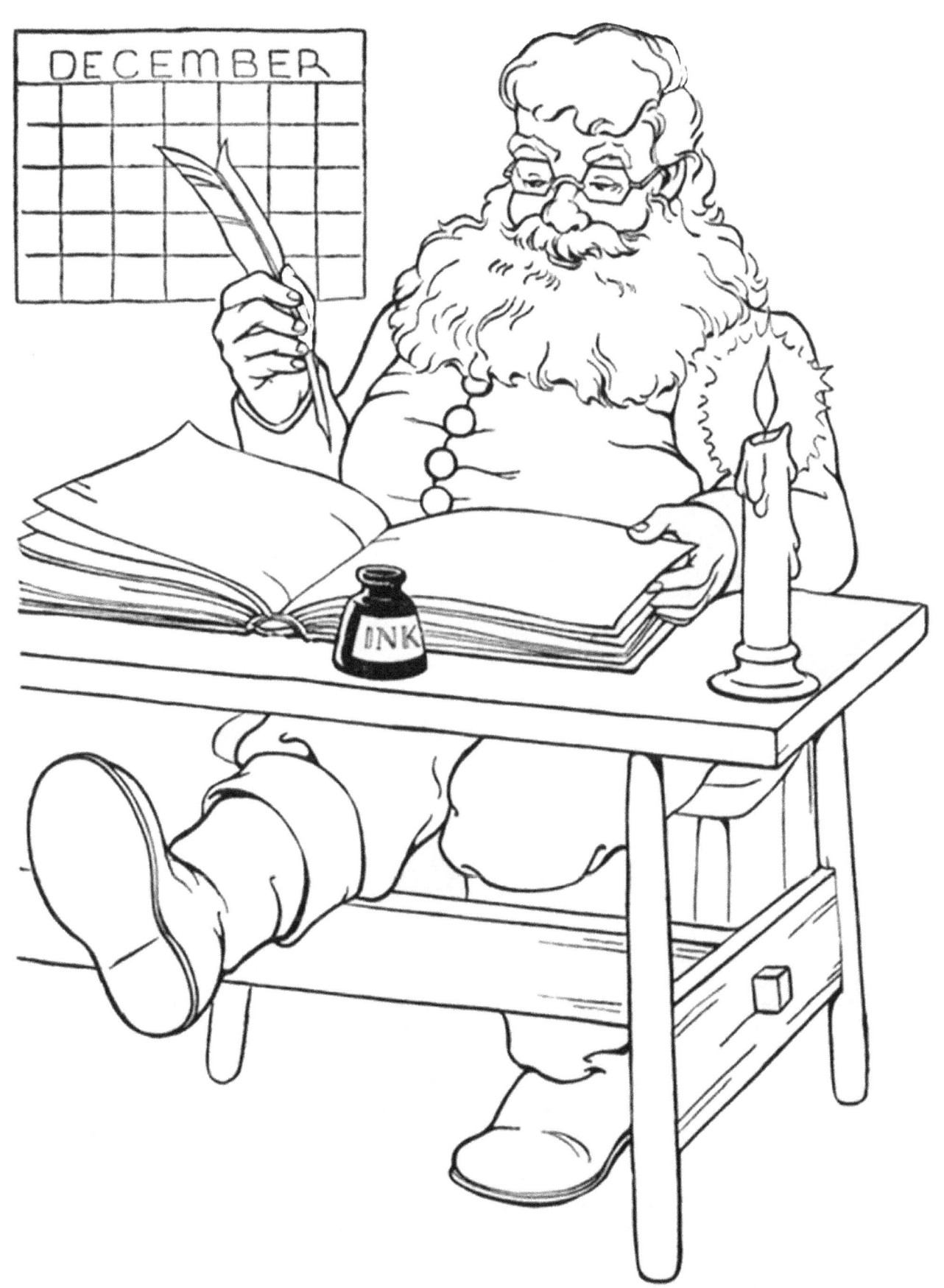

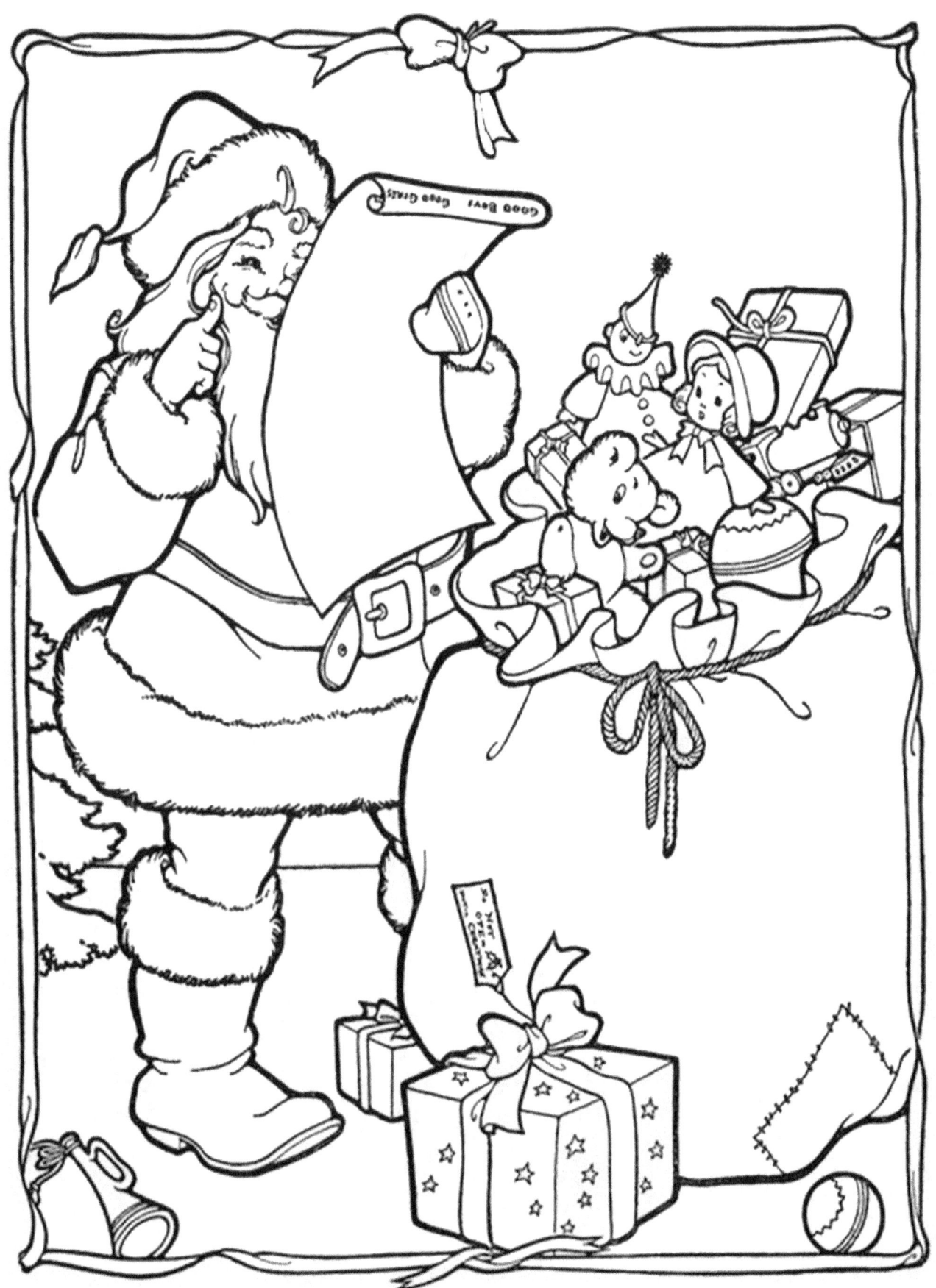

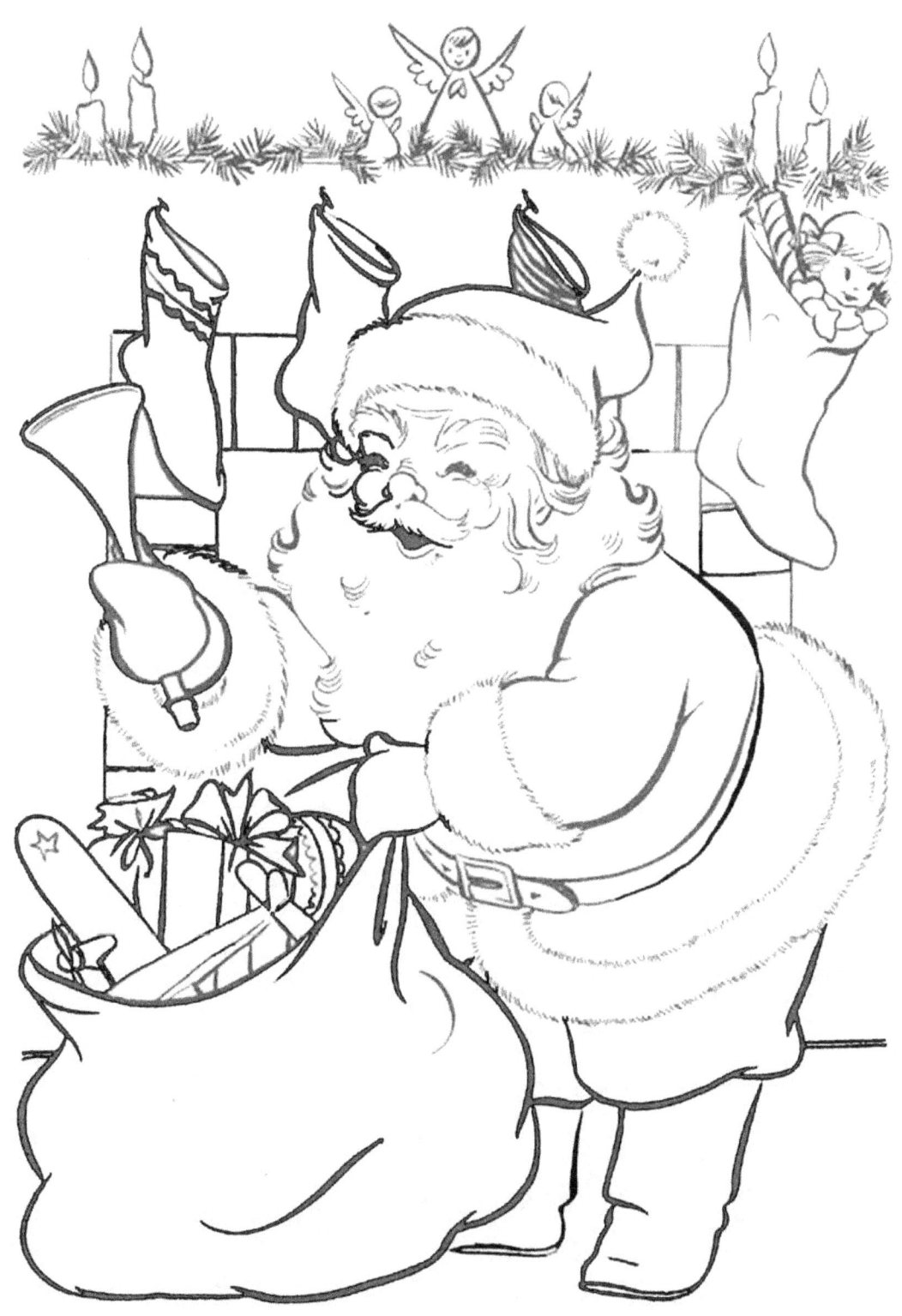

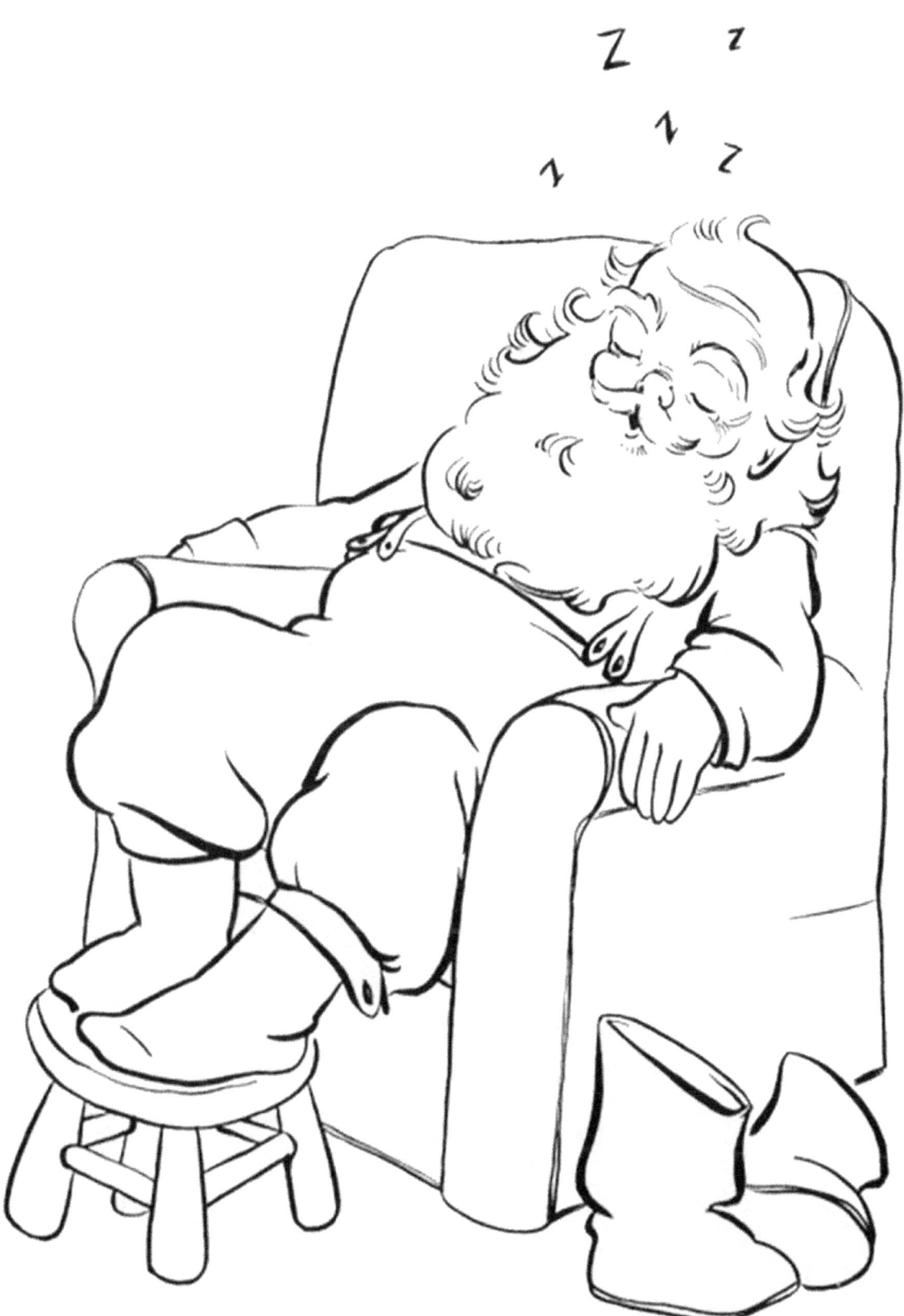

DECEMBER 24

SANTA'S LIST

NORTH POLE NEWS
DEC 24

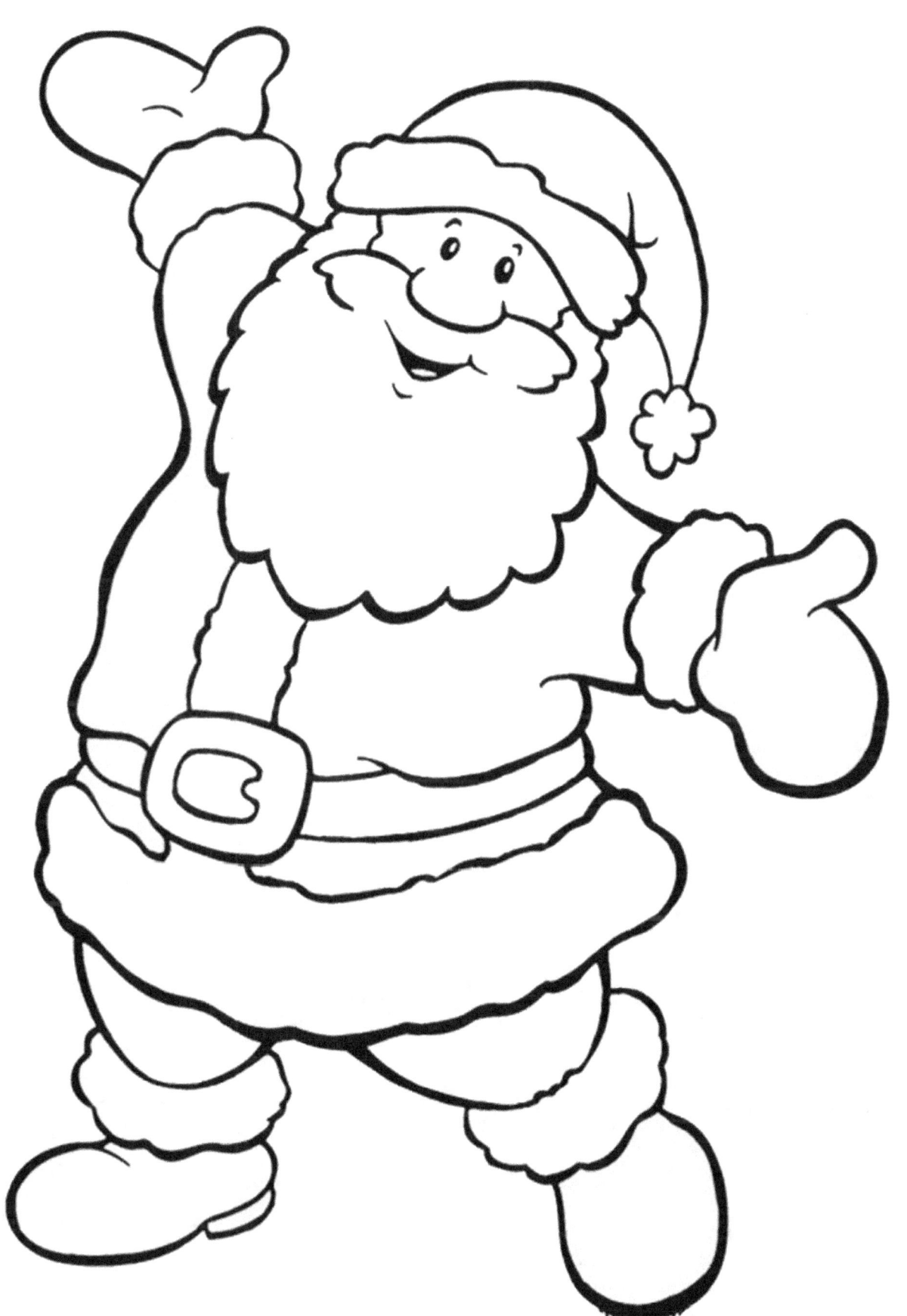

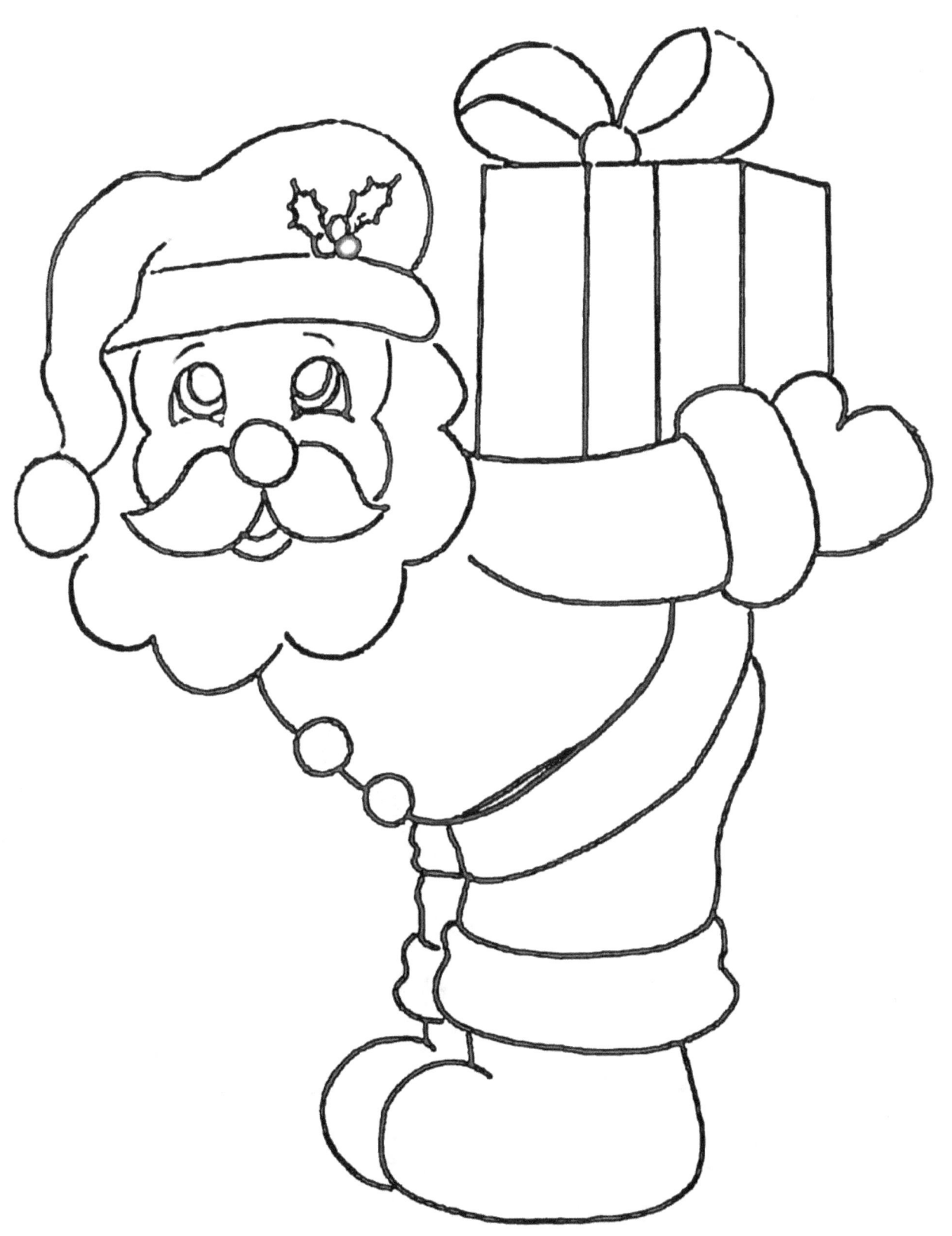

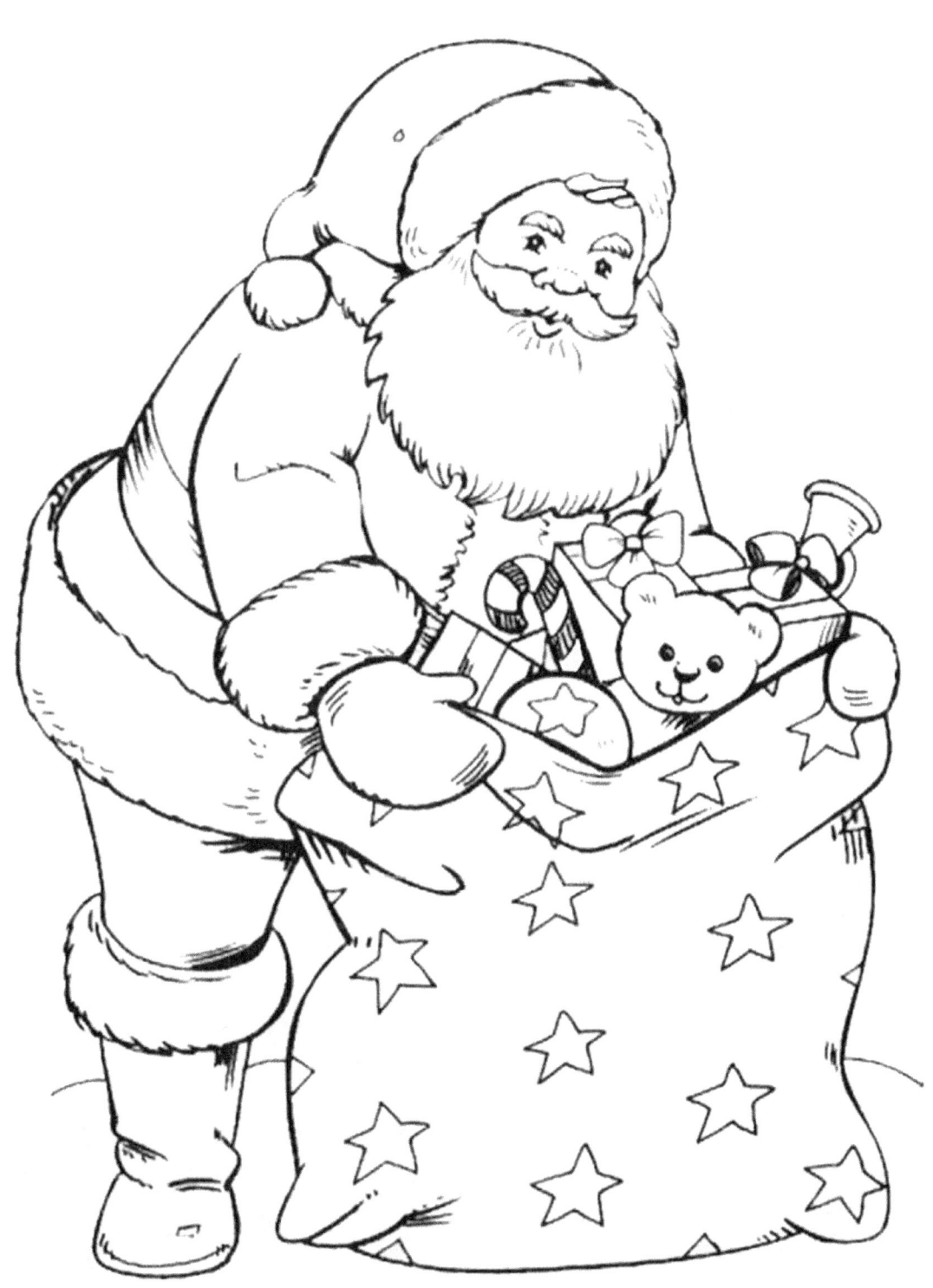

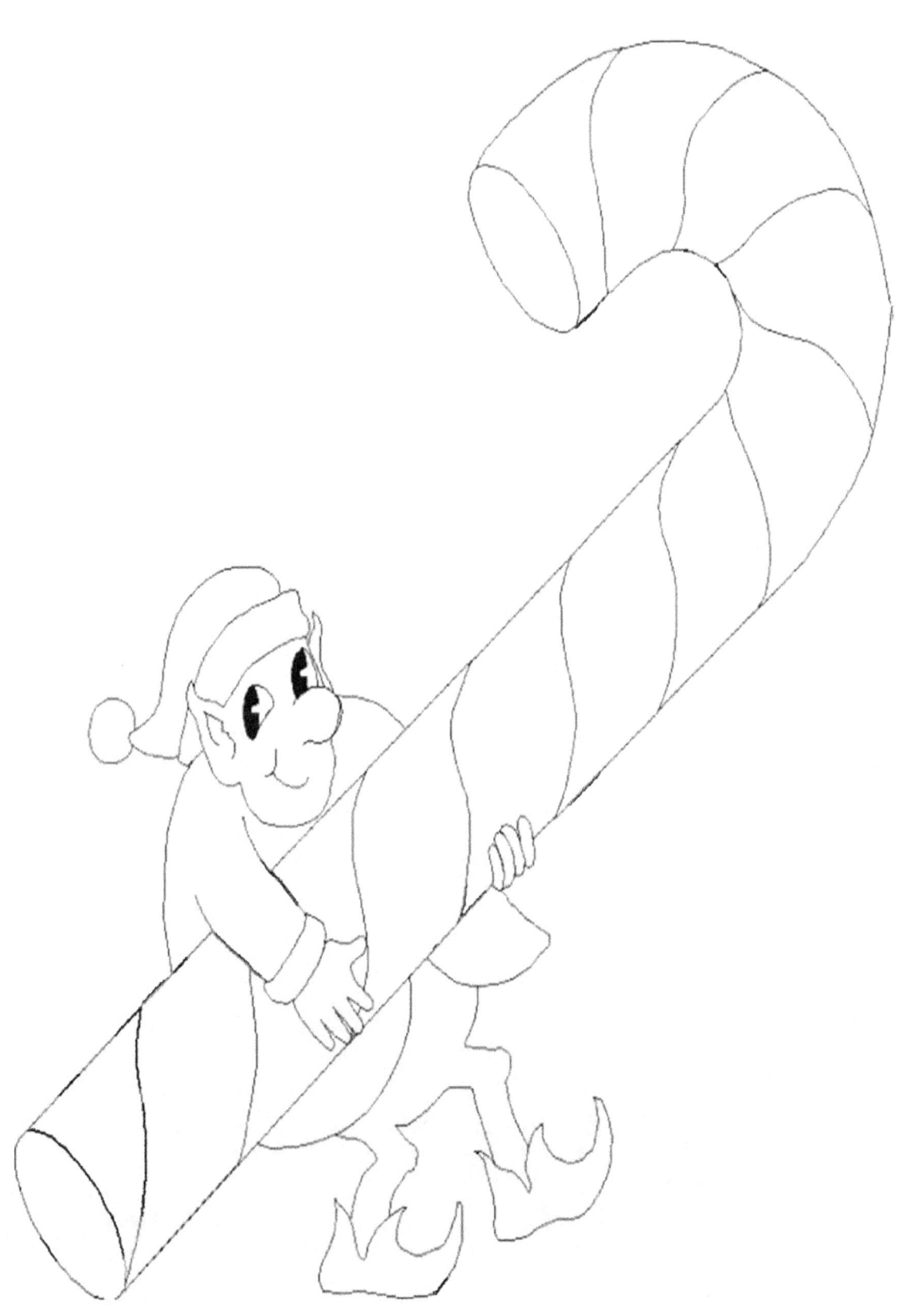

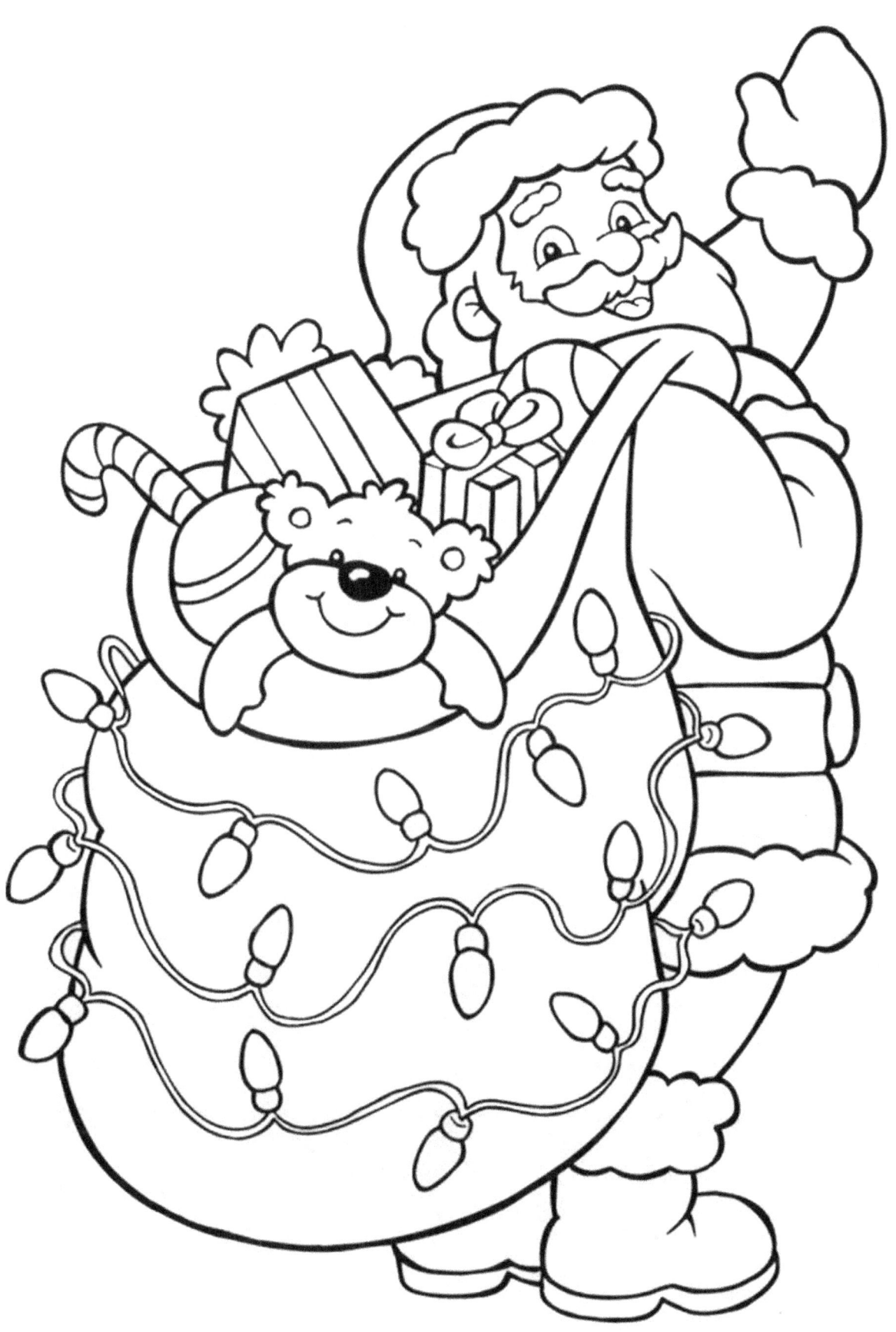

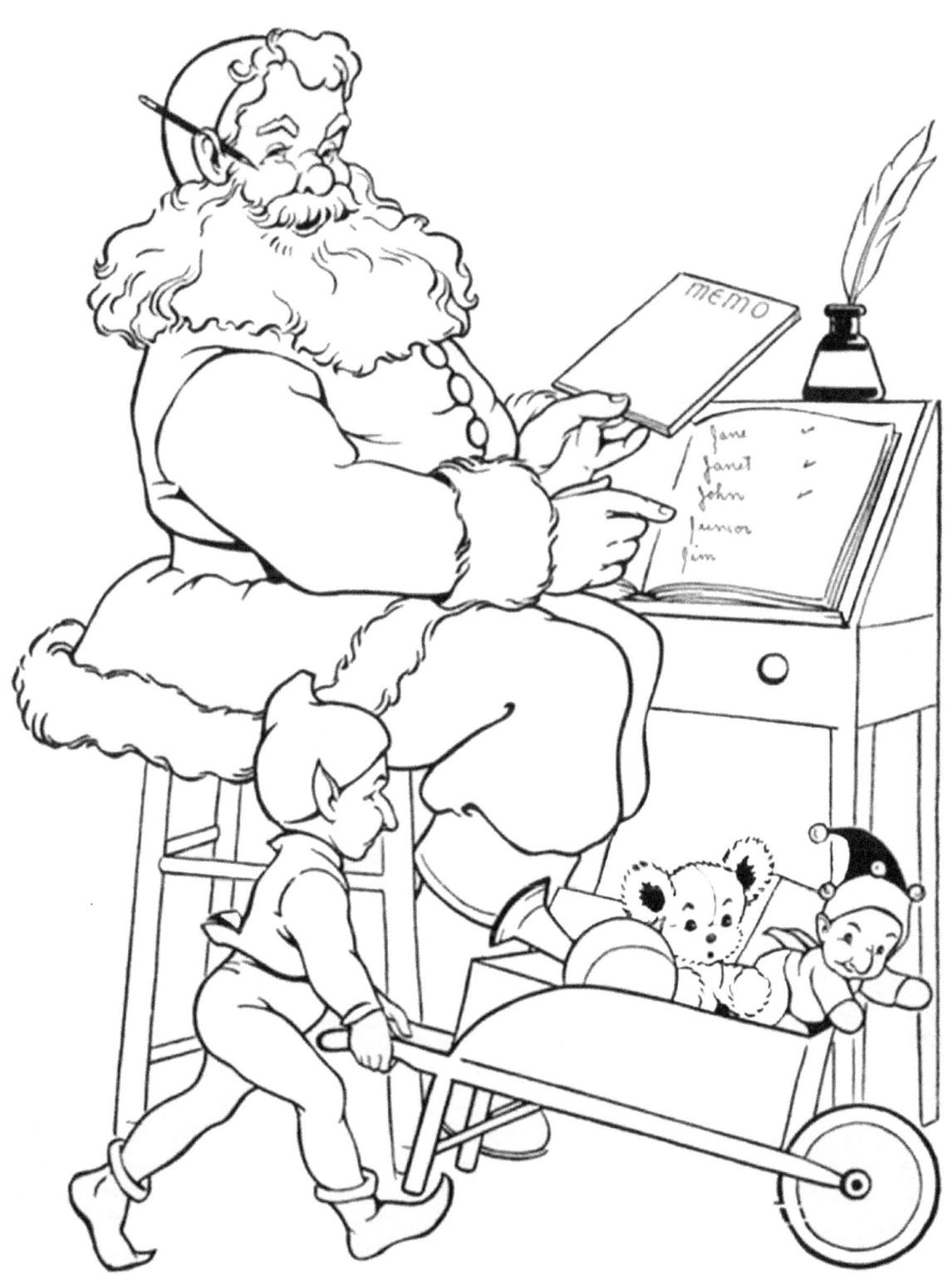

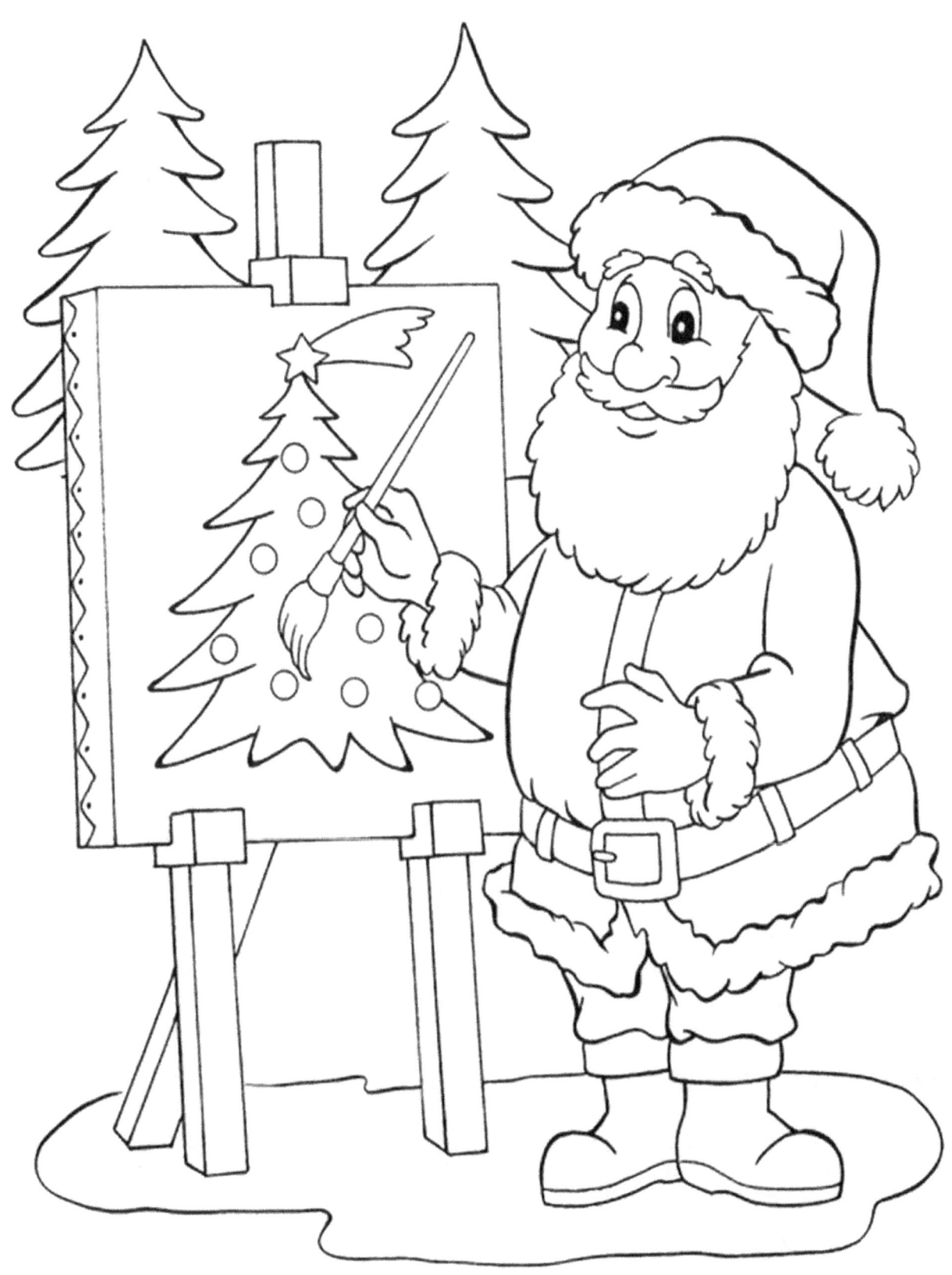

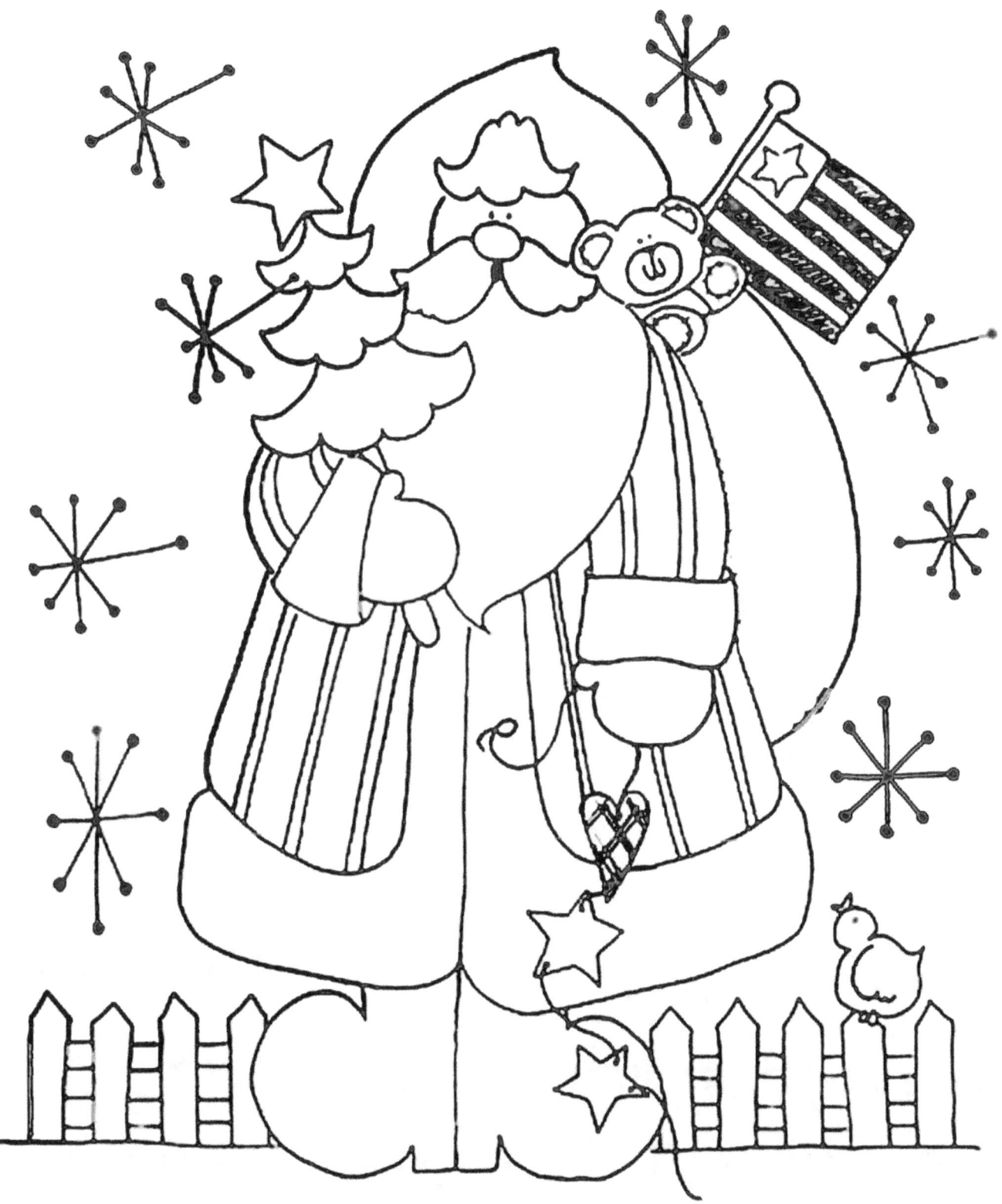

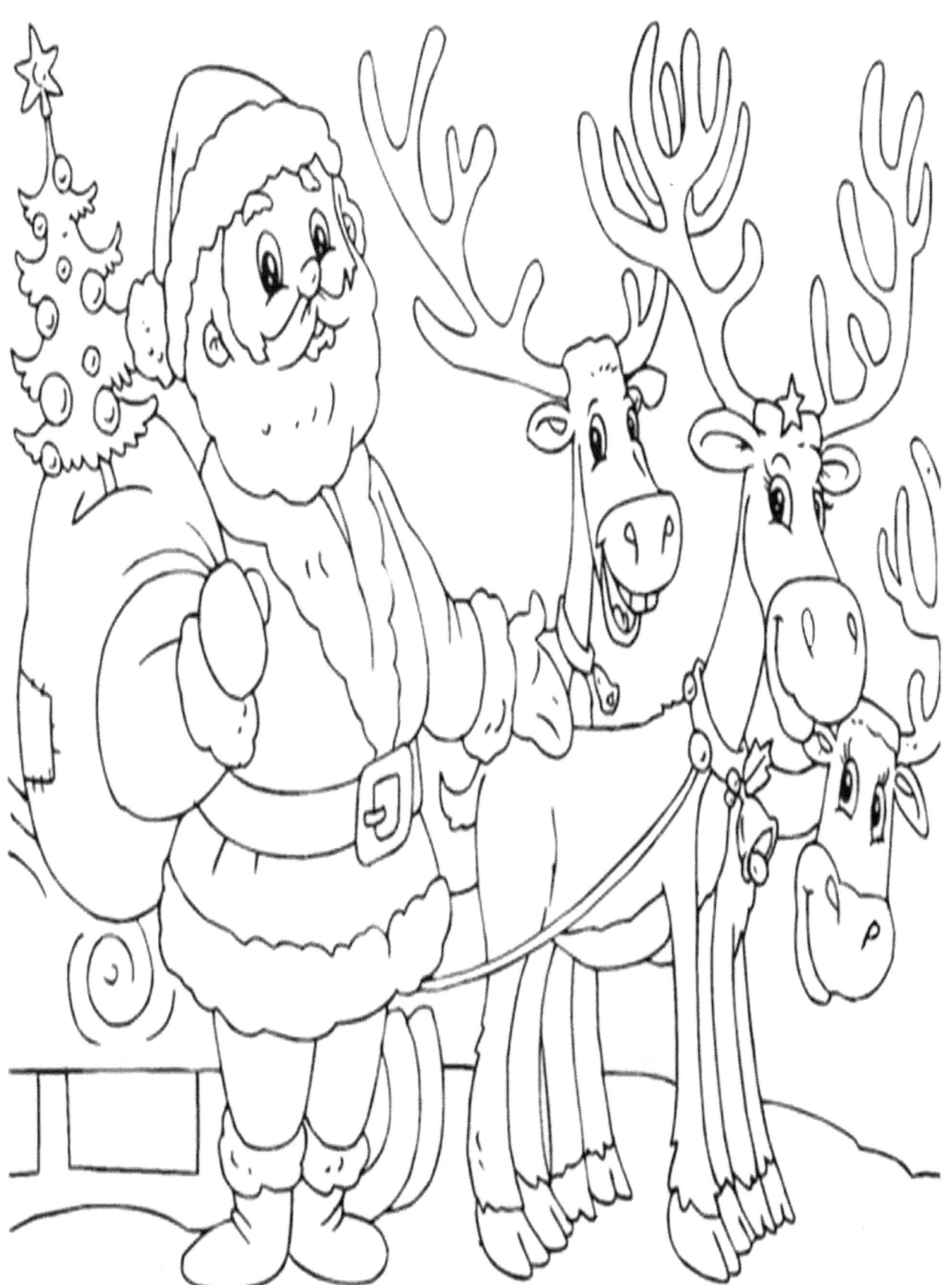

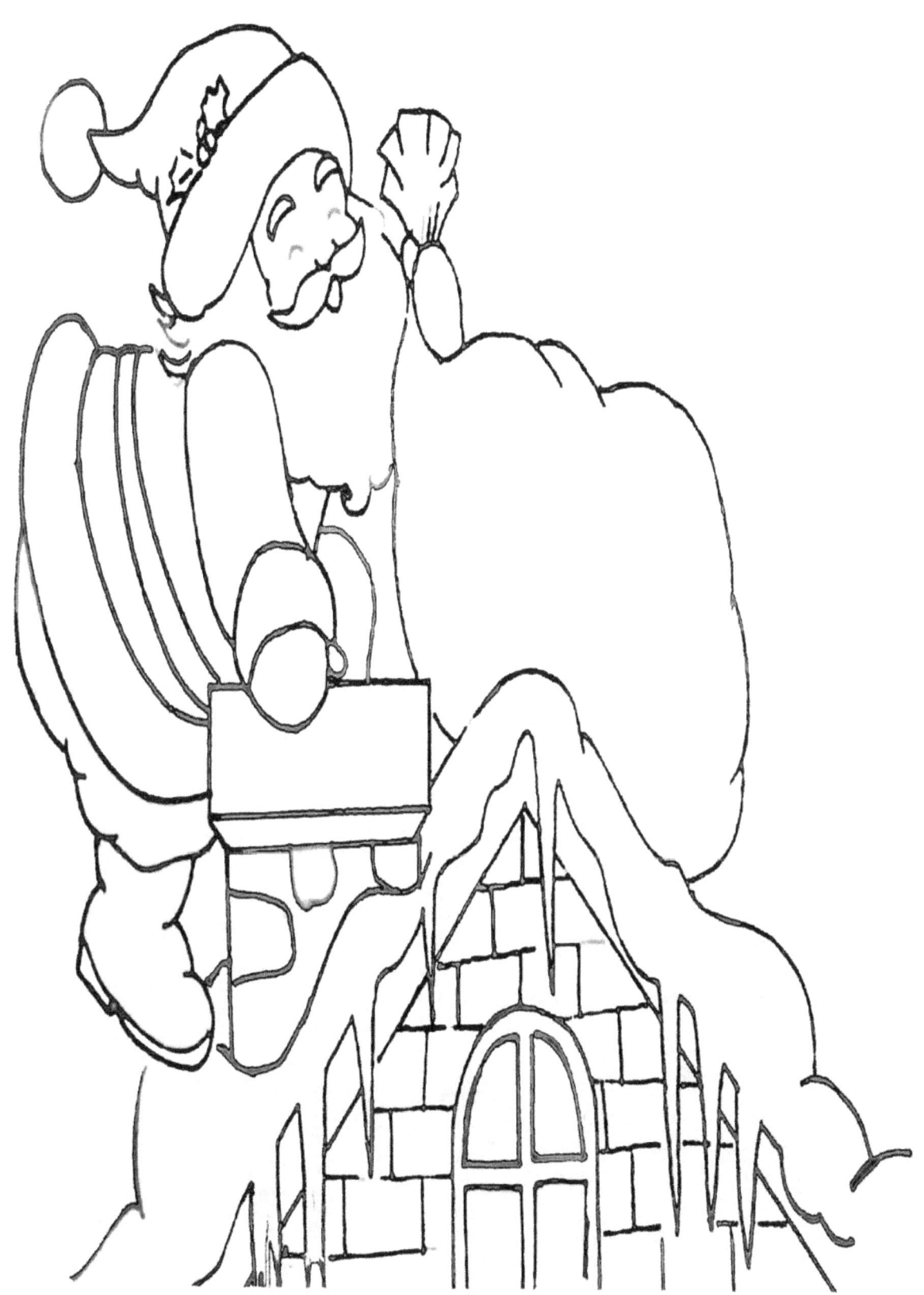

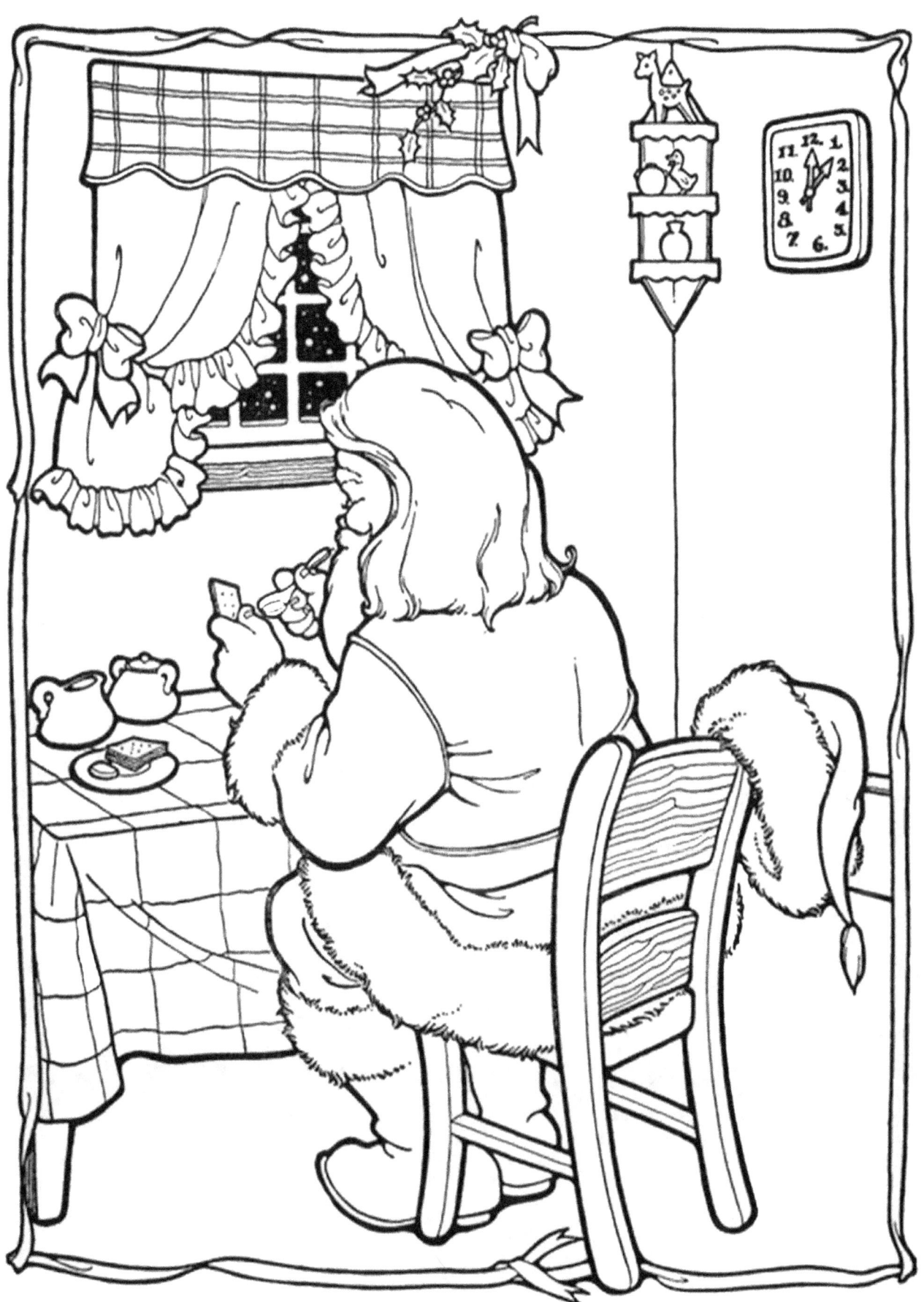

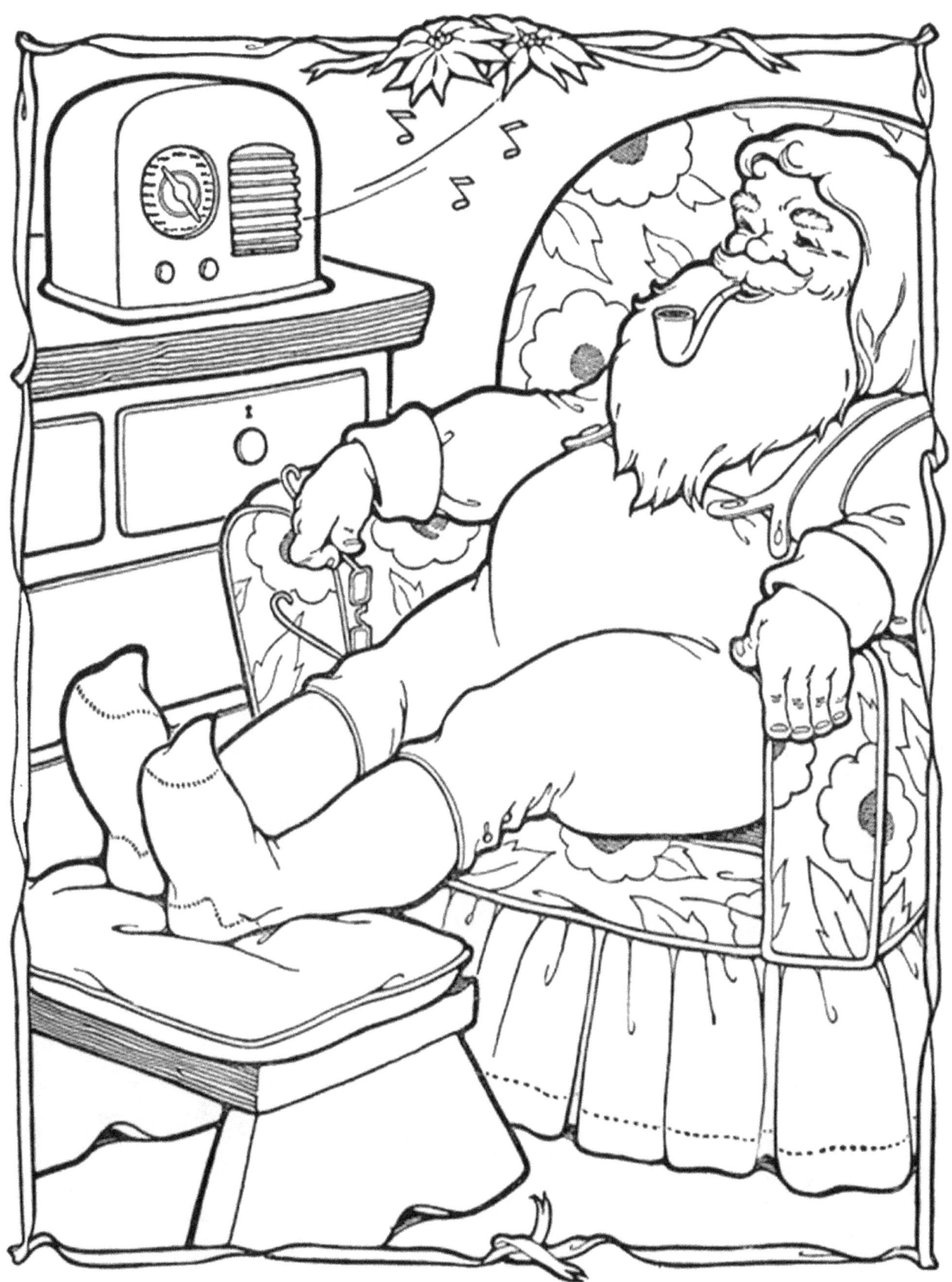

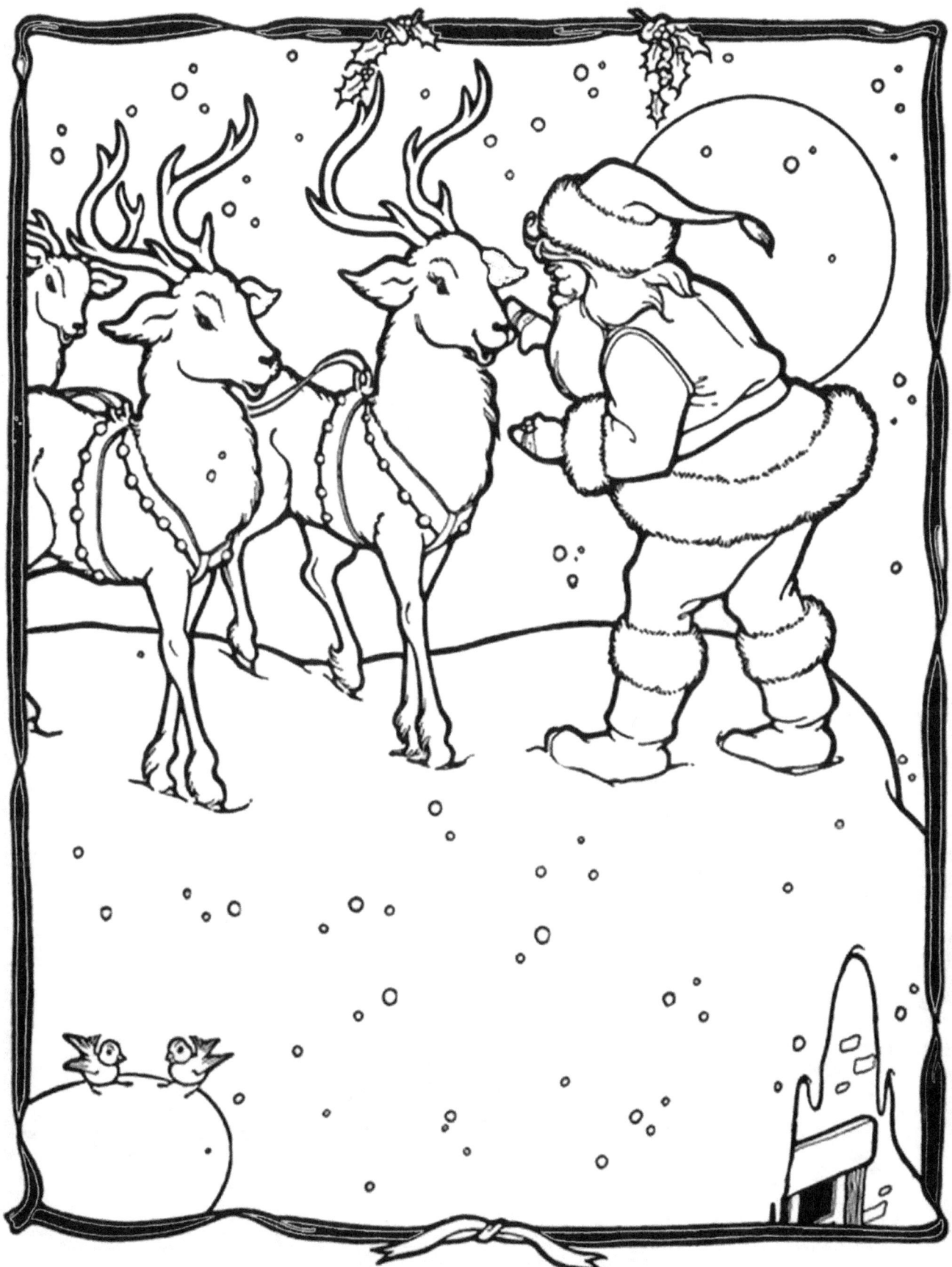

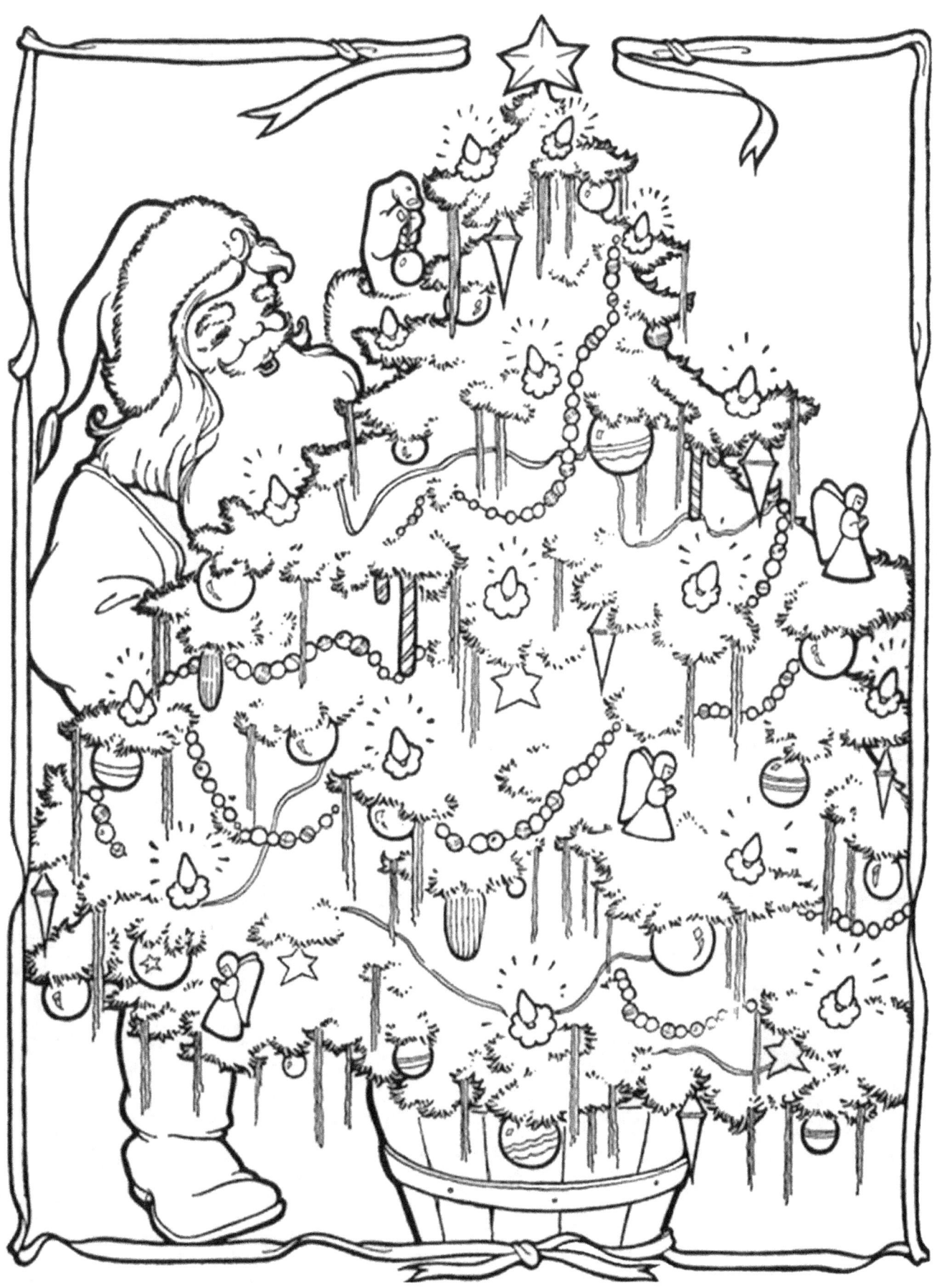

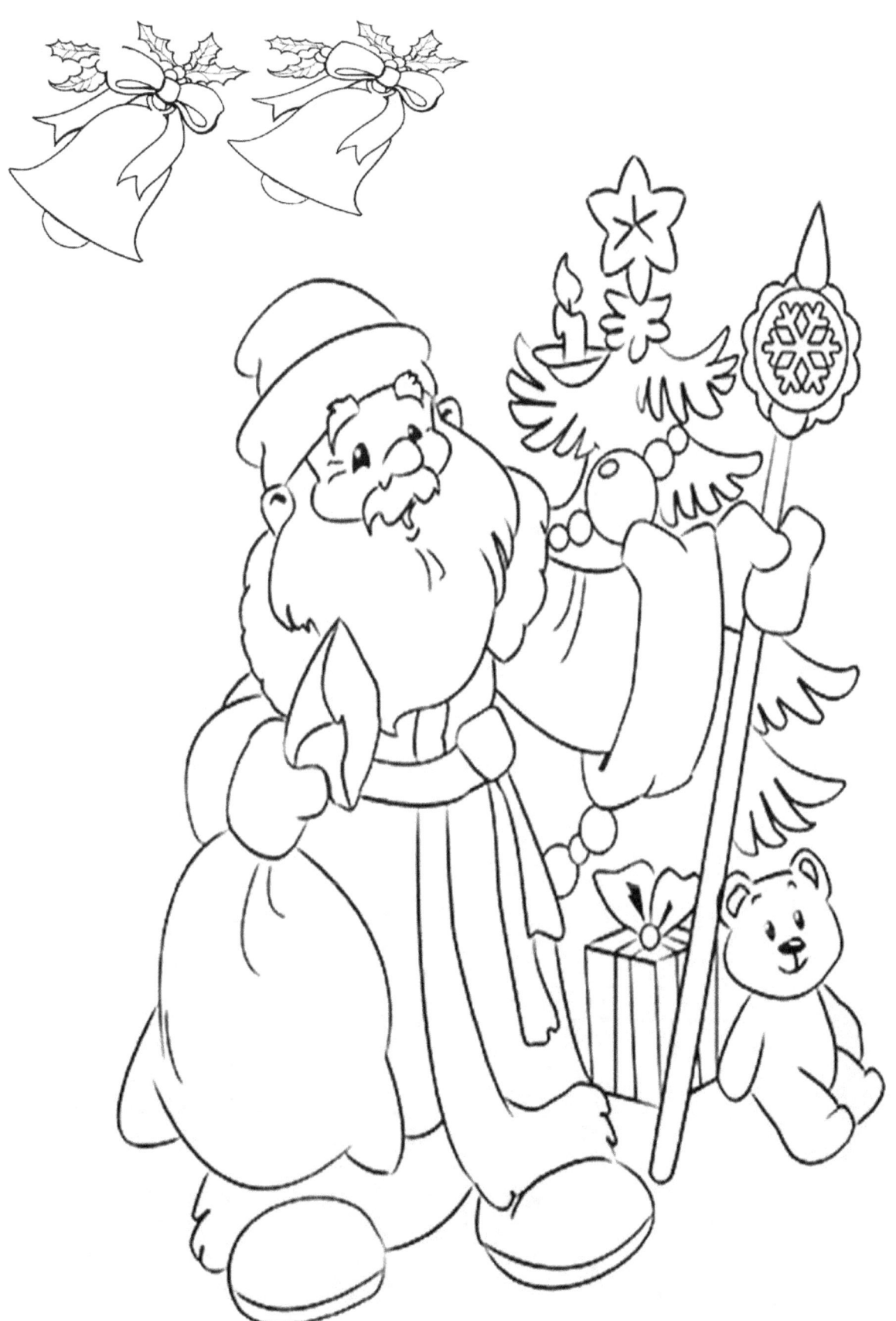

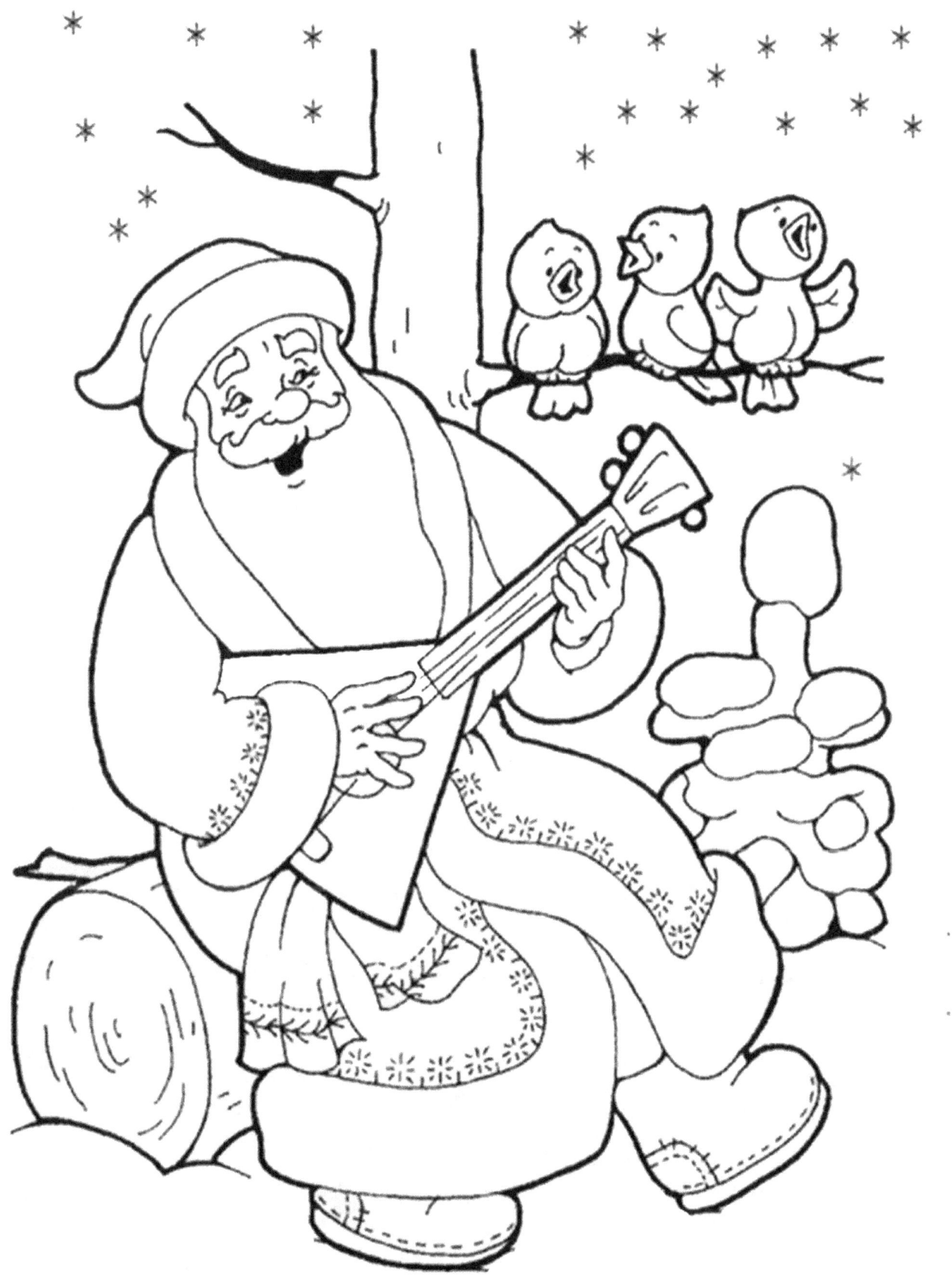

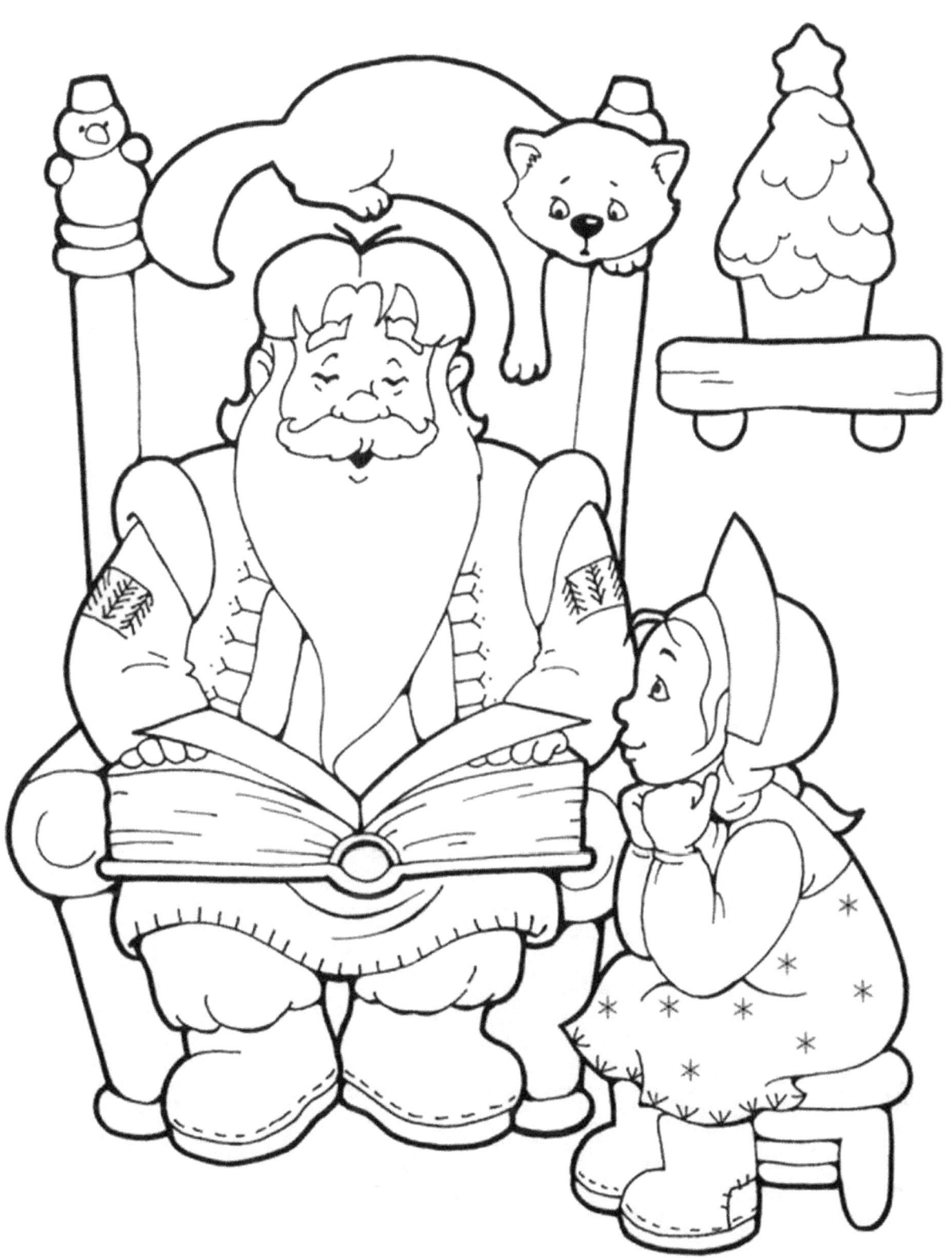

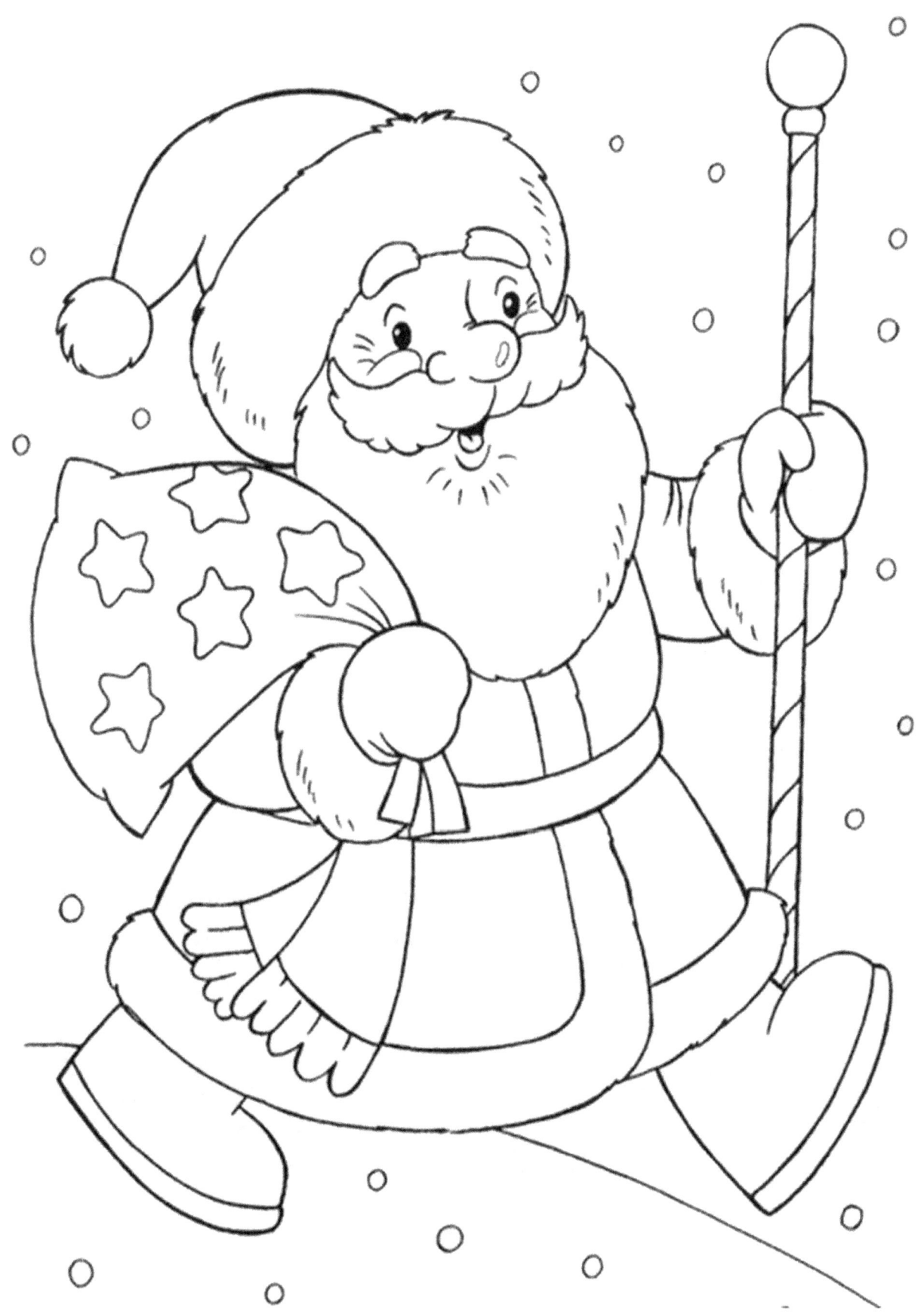

Thank You

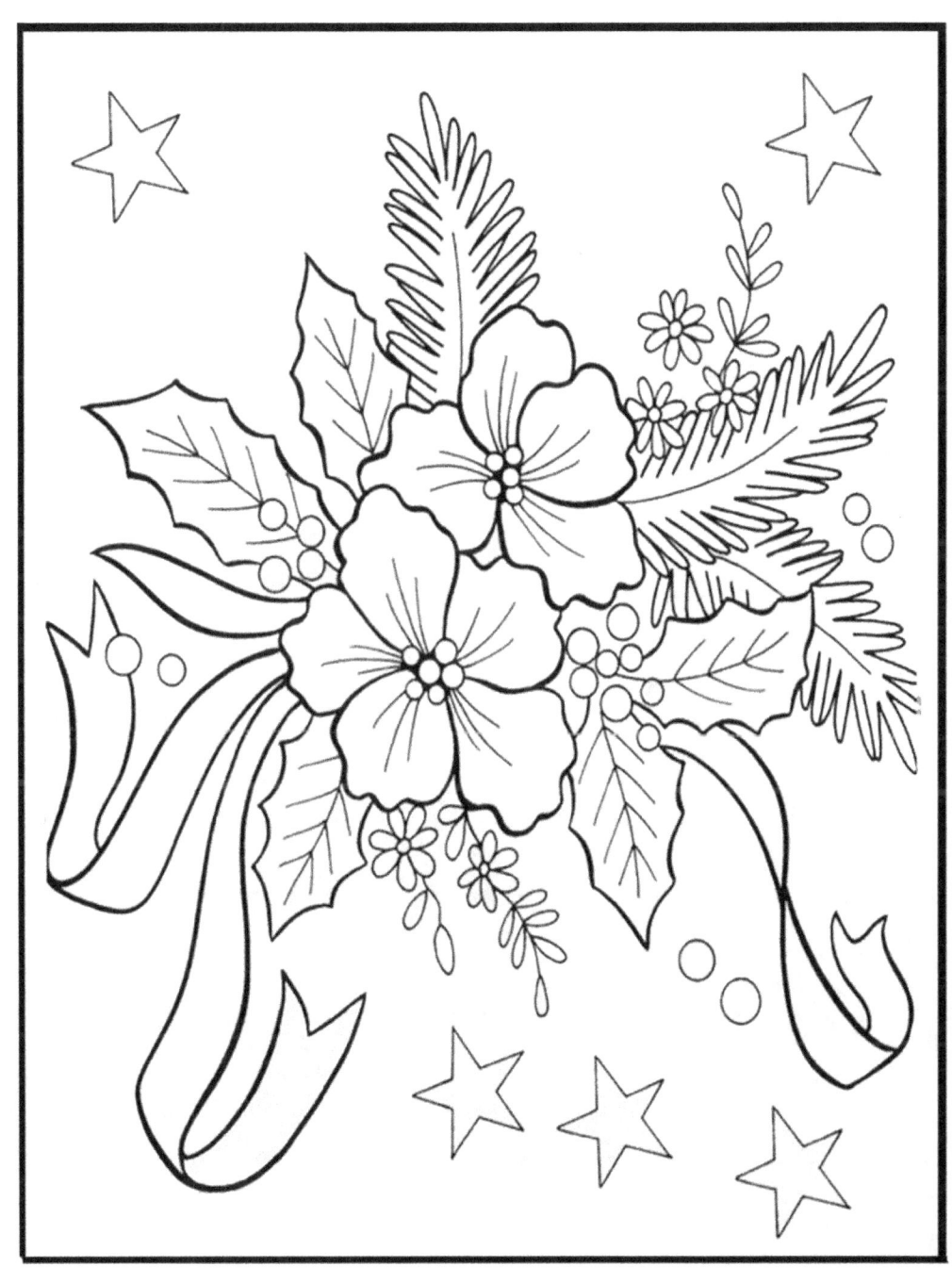